D1461461

FURTHER STEPS ON
A SPIRITUAL PATH

Also by White Eagle

A GUIDE TO LIVING WITH DEATH AND DYING

BEAUTIFUL ROAD HOME

FIRST STEPS ON A SPIRITUAL PATH

THE BOOK OF STAR LIGHT

THE GENTLE BROTHER

GOLDEN HARVEST

HEAL THYSELF

JESUS, TEACHER AND HEALER

THE LIGHT BRINGER

THE LIVING WORD OF ST JOHN

PRAYER, MINDFULNESS AND INNER CHANGE

THE PATH OF THE SOUL

THE QUIET MIND

SPIRITUAL UNFOLDMENT ONE

SPIRITUAL UNFOLDMENT TWO

SPIRITUAL UNFOLDMENT THREE

SPIRITUAL UNFOLDMENT FOUR

THE SOURCE OF ALL OUR STRENGTH

THE STILL VOICE

SUNRISE

TREASURES OF THE MASTER WITHIN

WALKING WITH THE ANGELS

WHITE EAGLE'S LITTLE BOOK OF HEALING COMFORT

WHITE EAGLE ON FESTIVALS AND CELEBRATIONS

WHITE EAGLE ON THE GREAT SPIRIT

WHITE EAGLE ON DIVINE MOTHER, THE FEMININE
AND THE MYSTERIES

WHITE EAGLE ON THE INTUITION AND INITIATION

WHITE EAGLE ON LIVING IN HARMONY WITH THE SPIRIT

Further Steps on a Spiritual Path

Wisdom from White Eagle

THE WHITE EAGLE PUBLISHING TRUST
NEW LANDS · LISS · HAMPSHIRE · ENGLAND

First published 1967 as WISDOM FROM WHIITE EAGLE
Republished under the present title, rearranged
and with new matter, February 2006

© The White Eagle Publishing Trust, 1967, 2006

British Library Cataloguing-in-Publication Data
A catalogue record for this book is available
from the British Library

ISBN 978-0-85487-170-4

Set in Spectrum at the Publisher and
printed in China by Artical Printing

CONTENTS

INTRODUCTION

A recent White Eagle book was given the title FIRST STEPS ON A SPIRITUAL PATH, and in the present volume we meet again a wise philosopher with a wonderful teaching for the new age. He leads us to an understanding of the 'real world', so different from the physical; to an understanding that death need bring no separation; and he offers above all love: love of the Being in whom we are all united as well as love of our neighbour, which brings healing deep within the soul of the individual and the soul of the world. He shows us the enormous spiritual potential we all have.

We are thus proud to present this edition, revised, expanded and much rearranged, of a book previously entitled simply WISDOM FROM WHITE EAGLE. It contains new teaching, as well as a large part of the contents of the previous edition, and a 'Moment of Reflection' to provide a focus at the end of each chapter. The teachings have been brought together in a way which brings White Eagle very close, and makes this book ideal for those who are new to his teaching. Reading it, we get a very real sense of the wisdom of this illumined teacher who first spoke through Grace Cooke.

White Eagle has never made claims for himself. When working through Grace Cooke and establishing the work of the White Eagle Lodge, he always described himself as a spokesman for a group. This group is known as the Star Brotherhood and their symbol is a shining six-pointed Star. The Star brethren (both male and female) are wise, illumined souls working from the higher spheres to help human kind towards a deeper understanding of the true brotherhood of all life, and to provide a way to see the light of God, or the Christ Light (to use a favourite term of White Eagle's) in every heart.

Those who work in White Eagle's name hope that this book will touch *your* heart as you read it, and that you will feel his presence at your side: a wise friend and helper who understands your need. He can lift you above the mists of earth into the sunshine of spiritual joy and enlightenment.

Jenny Dent
December 2005

I

IN THE BEGINNING

WE COME with love and peace, praying that our words will give you food for thought, and that we may be able to stimulate the spirit of the Son of God in your hearts. All humanity belongs to God. Some of God's children are very young, some are older; but as we look on humanity we see in all people a light shining like a jewel in the heart; we see the potential Christ self even in the least evolved.

In the beginning was the Word, and the Word was with God, and the Word was God.* In the beginning was light: all things are formed through light. If there were no light at all on earth, but only darkness, there would be no life. Light is sometimes called the 'Son' of God. 'The Son' means also the spiritual Sun; a spiritual sunlight existing within, behind and all around the sun. As the physical sun's rays continually pour down

**John 1 : 1*

on the earth, bestowing life and light and creating harmony in nature, harmony in the spheres, so the spiritual Sun gives life and light to the soul.

In the beginning, your Creator conceived the perfect life. He put humanity on this planet with certain knowledge; deep in human hearts the Creator implanted the key to the mysteries and the glory of life. But the pull of the earth has held humanity: physical matter pulled humanity down, to the extent that people became slaves to matter instead of remaining free. Stories have come down the ages about the various cataclysms, such as the story of Atlantis being submerged. Other continents have suffered in this manner; some you have never even heard of.

You do not even know the age of the earth. Indeed, you have no conception at all of the true nature of time or space. Scientists have certain methods of calculation and form their own theories, which are believed for a time and then disproved to make way for a new one. Truly you are unlikely to understand time and space until you develop spiritual perception, for the knowledge you seek comes only with unfolding and expanding consciousness.

As humanity evolves, the very substance of earth itself becomes brighter and more refined. A baby is born on earth powerless to help itself. So it is with the human spirit born or breathed forth from the heart of the Creator to become clothed in matter, unaware of its potentialities. The whole purpose of incarnation is this slow evolution of the spirit, beginning with its awakening in matter and going on through self-consciousness to God-consciousness. Spirit itself is pure. Spirit is the perfect seed from the heart of God, but the purpose of life on earth is gradually to develop the power of the spirit within.

God did more than give human kind this beautiful earth to live on, this beautiful body for the spirit to inhabit. Throughout the ages, He–She has sent messengers to help human kind. In the beginning, messengers came to this planet not only from the spirit world, but from other planets and from outer space—God-men and God-women, they are called. They came to bring the vision glorious; to offer knowledge of the universal and celestial life.

They imparted knowledge of the spiritual laws governing life on earth. Some followed the wisdom teaching of these 'God-beings,' or 'Sun-men and -women' but others, as they began to know their power, wanted to dominate others. This eventually caused disturbances and even catastrophes, and much suffering. Nevertheless, the loving, beneficent Power always came to the rescue, gathering into the fold those who were truly trying to follow and obey spiritual law. They were cared for and protected, and only those who deliberately turned their backs on the light had to follow a path of pain.

You cannot conceive the vast space of time occupied by this development, or the slow growth of earth and earth's humanity. If we speak of millions of years, it means nothing; eternity is beyond the comprehension of the finite mind. Nevertheless, even if it is beyond your power to see the picture as a whole, it is interesting to look back into the past in order to get a glimpse of the spiritual evolution of humanity.

When a man or woman has attained pure spiritual consciousness, for a time he or she appears to lose all contact with earth. He or she may journey to other worlds, other planets, and meet congenial friends and companions known on earth. He or she may live there for a time in perfect happiness.

Yet such individuals do not sever themselves entirely from earth. Many of those illumined ones, White Brothers, visit groups on earth working for the enlightenment of human kind.

The Silent Watchers

We bring you love and joy and peace. We would raise your consciousness so that you become aware of the presence of the Shining Ones. We would help you to open your hearts to the presence of the Great Watchers and hear in your hearts the message they bring. There are many initiates, many elder brethren; but there are twelve Great Masters, the Silent Watchers, who have humanity in their care, and who are active in their work with humanity.

You often hear reference to the Masters, and to the Great White Lodge. The Great White Lodge consists of these true initiates. They are full of love; they care for themselves not one iota; their whole object is to help humanity. Some masters remain passive behind the scenes, yet they are ever active in thought. There are those who are active with humanity, working with organizations and groups striving for the progress of human life.

If we can, we would give a glimpse of the meaning of the Great White Lodge and the great Masters. We would give you a wider conception than you may previously have held to help the development of your own psychic and spiritual gifts. Think of the first great cause, the Sun, and see, if you can, emanating from it the seven rays, the seven colours of the spectrum. Now see how the rays from the Sun, or this 'first principle', permeate all life. Each ray is connected with the Sun and one of the seven planets, and all work within humanity for the evolution, growth and gradual perfecting of the individual soul. In thinking of the great masters, try to go beyond the limitations of human personality to a great being at the head of one of these rays of human knowledge and development. Get a broader vision and remember also that there are other systems, other suns, other universes; yet all are linked, all part of the whole.

There are many movements in the world, all doing fine work. Such groups and organizations—yes, and religions—are helped in their work by the initiates of the Great White Lodge above. There are other avenues of service too, such as art, music, drama and literature. All creative work for the upliftment of the human soul is guided and inspired by master souls. Anyone ready to respond to the pure selfless influence of a master sounds a note in the white ether. The master hears, and a response comes unfailingly. However, these great ones do not always work in direct contact with the earth people; they use their disciples and those you know as spirit guides to convey their message. You ask how you can be sure that the message comes from a true source. To ring true, it must be of the same calibre as the Christ message; it must be pure, selfless, kind and just. In sending you guidance, the master will always speak with love, and direct your thoughts towards goodwill and peace; he or she will never encourage you to antagonism, never to self-aggrandizement, but will always lead you towards humility, loving kindness, and co-operation with all creatures.

You will be able to unfold the power that enables you to recognize an elder brother on the astral plane by your practice of meditation and the development of discernment. People long to see a master, to feel a physical touch from him or her, and to hear a master's voice. But the aspirant has to qualify spiritually in order to recognize elder brethren on the astral plane, which is a very real plane of consciousness, and indeed more substantial than your own world.

We have merely touched upon the seven Silent Watchers at the head of the seven rays. Yes, the grand company of the White Brotherhood is countless because there are many great souls, great beings who have under their command many messengers, disciples and students. This vast company consists of every soul who has developed true love, and gives true service to God and human kind. All those who aspire to work with the Light and to bring the Light to earth are recognized as brethren of the Light, and are numbered among the White Brothers.*

Travelling Together

You are not alone on your evolutionary path. You travel in company. We speak of the White Brotherhood, Brothers of the Star, Sisters of the Light, call them what you will. Wherever a group is formed of men and women who are strictly obeying the law of brotherhood, in order to give love and service; wherever the spirit of true brotherhood is established and forms a nucleus, it attracts the attention of the brethren invisible who will work behind the scenes to help on the work. They will never withdraw their aid

*In an early book called THE OPEN DOOR, White Eagle's medium Grace Cooke explained the term 'the White Brotherhood' as describing 'the Brethren in spirit of the Great White Light'. She further compared the Brothers with 'they which came out of great tribulation, and have washed their robes, and made them white in the blood of the lamb', here quoting the Revelation of St John. They are not, of course, necessarily male.

unless the spiritual power is dissipated by the group's own wilfulness. The Brothers and Sisters come to earth again and yet again in physical form. They move among their pupils, usually unrecognized. Only when the disciples have been tested and have learnt obedience to the Law are they able to receive the visit of an elder brother–sister in full consciousness.

Would you recognize a master or elder brother if he or she spoke to you in a public place, or if he or she sat beside you in a public vehicle? In all probability not. When Jesus met the disciples on the road to Emmaus, the disciples did not recognize him. They walked and talked with this perfectly ordinary person and, thinking him to be a stranger, asked him if he had heard about the crucifixion of the man Jesus.

We want you to understand that in the world of spirit we work in groups and each personality in the group has his or her own special contribution to make to the whole. We who speak to you are a group of white brethren who are all as one spirit, completely in harmony one with another.

When an important conference takes place between the leaders of the nations, for example, to most of you it is just a worldly conference; but we would assure you that no such conference affecting the destiny of humanity works alone; it is watched over, guided and inspired by a spiritual company. It is helped—if it will be helped—by what I can only describe as a Grand Council in the higher worlds, whose members are quite untouched by the entanglements of earthly mind, the influences of the astral planes, or planes of desire. The Council we speak of comes from the Great White Lodge. It has to accord with divine law, but as with you on earth it has a certain amount of freewill; it does not have to work entirely by rule of thumb. It can influence the younger brethren on the earth, but much depends on the state of mind of the people concerned.

We would have you understand that every individual soul is linked to another as in a chain, from earth to the loftiest heights. You can receive communications and messages from these highly-advanced White Brothers. Step by step the message comes down. As we speak to you now, another influence behind is using us to convey certain truths to you; behind him there is yet another—and so on through the spheres. Every one of you has your own guide, as well as your guardian angel, and you can be helped beyond all your dreams if you will go with a humble spirit into the inner sanctuary and pray, not in a self-pitying way but humbly; not for self-gratification but that you may fit yourself to be a true servant of humanity. You have before you the examples of the great ones who have served humanity all through the ages. This is the way of life, to live not only to enjoy yourselves but to beautify, to benefit earth, to help forward the spiritual evolution of all life. The responsibility rests on each one; on the individual soul the whole community depends.

A MOMENT OF REFLECTION

Using your natural power of imagination, come with us right into the world of light, into the temple built with loving, faithful hearts and faith in God as the Creator. There we stand in the vast company of shining beings, the saints of all time. We have to thank them for their service to us, for the saints are slowly but surely raising all creation into a heavenly state to become brothers and sisters of the light. The way is shown to us all, embodied or disembodied; the way of service. Before us lies this shining path.

II

A GREATER POWER
KNOWS OUR TRUE NEED

FROM THE SOURCE of life, impulses radiate throughout the universe. Permeating all life are these pulsations, these forces, some of which are called positive and others negative. Now you are a sensitive instrument and through spiritual development and unfoldment you are training yourself to react to these forces in a correct and balanced way, not allowing yourself to be pulled too much one way or another. You are learning to keep on a steady path of light; to become a perfectly-balanced soul. You are learning to become like a master: one who is perfectly balanced, one who reacts in the right and balanced way to all the influences which play on him or her.

Try to realize that you are not the little you that you think you are, but part of a more beautiful soul than you can conceive. That soul is your higher self.

Only a small part of you is manifesting through your body, but there is something within you, your inner self, attached at all times to that greater Self that is separate from, but is also part of, God. This Self will be almost beyond your realization at present. In time, however, you will attain the enfolding truth and beauty of that higher Self, that higher life.

All men and women are linked, consciously or unconsciously, with the Supreme Power, God, and this is why they have the urge to pray for help from an unknown source, a higher power. It is natural even from childhood for people to reach out to something they can love and believe in and respect; and when the child grows older, even if he or she has become what you may call a materialist, there are times of crisis when he or she instinctively calls out to God.

While in incarnation you seem to be bound in darkness and limitation, unaware of the blazing guiding Star that is above you and linked to your heart. You cannot see the Silent Watchers who watch over you during your earthly journey, and you do not understand how closely you are cared for, how you are guided. Did not the Master Jesus say of the sparrows, *One of them shall not fall on the ground without your Father?** And

*Matthew 10 : 29–30

again, *the very hairs of your head are all numbered?* But you forget these words of wisdom when you are held fast by your own particular little anxiety; you become filled with trepidation and let these things control and even obsess you. If only you could remember the assurance made to you by the Son that your Father knows your need; that your Creator has so planned your life that only ultimate good awaits you, not ultimate pain and sorrow! You will learn in time to have faith in your Creator, for experience will teach you that good comes out of every bitter experience and that nothing is as bad as you fear.

Try to remember what we say. We speak to some who, we know, are in special need of comfort, encouragement and reassurance. Be sure, my child, that your Father in Heaven knows your need. What is happening to you has come to mould your character and bring beauty into your life. You may think we are over-optimistic. But we have every reason to be optimistic because our vision goes beyond your own, and we see that all is well.

All through your life, a guiding power watches over you; but it rests with you yourself whether you act in accordance with that guidance or whether you will turn your face away, act foolishly, and go over to the darkness—or, in old-fashioned language, Satan. But Satan is only another word for Saturn, the tester, and even the negative force is slowly and painfully working in life to test and purify you, and eventually bring you wisdom, bring you light.

Evidence

One day you will realize that you are surrounded, not only by spirit worlds and beings, but by finer physical or semi-physical worlds inhabited by people similar to yourself. Mingling with you sometimes are spirits not of this world but from other planets. It is not unknown for spirits from other planets to speak through a sensitive human instrument. Men and women are set in their ideas, and cannot get away from a one-track mind. But beyond that one-track mind are so many wonderful things, a glorious life of which you know nothing.

You find life difficult and lonely, and you feel as though you are always toiling; your feet are heavy and the road along which you drive yourself grows very hard. But learn to open your vision and have courage to believe what you want to believe. So many have said to us, 'O White Eagle, I wish I could believe! Give me proof and I will believe!' My dear child, the proof you cry out for is within you! You want to be assured that you are an eternal being, and that your Creator is all love? You want to know that there is nothing to fear in death? You want to know that you can never be separated from those you love? The answer to every question lies within your own being. You want to be sure that in your meditations you are not deluding yourself; that you are not just imagining something which looks very nice but is really only wispy and fantastic. When you rise in consciousness in your meditations and aspirations to your Creator, you become aware of something that is adorable and lovely. Oh, the breath of the Infinite! The perfume of that breath! Oh, the joy of that life! Is it real or is it something which will disappear in the morning?

We answer that all that is holy, all that is pure and sweet and lovely is of God, and it is real. That is your real state of life. Hearing this, you will say, 'Why then are we down here imprisoned in this heavy body? Why has the world fallen to its present state if human life aeons ago was so beautiful? If this world was ever a Garden of Eden, what has happened to it since? What have we done to bring about this terrible state of existence?' Yes, what have you done? What are you doing now? That is more to the point. Because if you lived every moment in the consciousness of your Creator, in the consciousness of the Son of God, the Christ, you would no longer be battened down in darkness; nor would you suffer. That love of God and of the spiritual life is creative and will create beauty and harmony in your body, in your life, and in your surroundings. It will give you a spiritual life that cannot be scarred or hurt, darkened or sullied by the illusory selfish existence.

You may look at life from your earthly level and see nothing but chaos. You say, 'What a muddle life is! What a terrible state the world is in!' Yet divine law operates only for good, brings beauty and harmony into manifestation at the lowest level, which is physical matter. While material life may appear chaotic, it is ever evolving. If you trace any work from its beginning, you will see that at first it goes through a period of chaos. For example, one sees confusion when a building is being constructed. When a painter begins, his canvas will be a baffling mixture of colour and unfinished form. Or you may see the overwritten pages of a book in preparation, and they will appear chaotic.

So in the course of spiritual and physical evolution, chaos may appear to reign, and those who do not know will say, 'Oh, men and women are so bad and there is so much evil in the world!' We would give you a vision, not of confusion and evil, but of an infinite power working in perfect order, from the heights to the depths, from heaven above right down to the physical and through all humanity. We would show you a process in all life of changing darkness into light. Light creates life. And even in the very lowest form of life, light is working amid the darkness. Divine law, the law of God, is working on evil, the positive state working on the negative, in a process that is gradually producing the perfect God-conscious being.

'Man–woman made perfect': these simple words express the whole truth. The light comes from heaven and dwells in the darkness; it works on the darkness—that is, on evil—and slowly, by an exact law and with perfect precision, creates the perfect form, the perfect soul, the perfect manifestation of the Son of God.

All over the earth can be found relics of great sun temples, and scientists puzzle their brains to work out how the ancients could have carried monster stones weighing many tons and built temples of them. The ancients knew the power of sound and rhythm; they understood this power and put it into operation. In some instances, they built their temples of etheric matter and light; and with the passing of time and the closing-down of human spiritual powers they solidified into stone. If you go to Stonehenge at certain times and open your inner vision you will see great angels there, the ancient ones, great ones from other planets whose power is centred there. Do you not see that creation is not a phenomenon confined to earth, or any one planet? It is cosmic in scope and all parts of it are one: there is constant interchange and intercommunication. In past ages, God-beings have come to earth. And so, in time, when the Lord God thinks it is good, and the earth people are ready, beings from outer space will come again and be seen and recognized by humanity, and they will bring great happiness to earth people.

The time will surely come when scientists, through their discoveries in the realms of physical science, will be faced with the truth that there is a spiritual as well as a physical universe. And when human kind discovers the wisdom of studying spiritual science, humanity will enter the most wonderful, the most beauteous world, for in doing so all will quite plainly see the true way of life, and will naturally develop all the Godlike qualities that are within.

You may think this lies a long way in the future; but if humanity passes this present test, and we think it will, human kind will then advance on that path of spiritual unfoldment, on all the various rays of development—the ray of science, of philosophy, education, occultism, art, music, healing and so on—and the influence of the great ones at the head of all these rays will be directed in full power upon human kind.

Life begins from the centre, from spirit, and radiates in ever-increasing circles or cycles of life, growing ever more perfect.

Expanding Vision

In communications from the world of spirit, much may seem incomprehensible to you because, closed as you are in a finite state of life, you can only think in terms of three dimensions. When you have learned to live and work in harmony with divine law you will be freed from all limitations; you will be liberated from earth, not by death of the body, but because you have learnt to master matter. When the soul has attained complete mastery over matter, over the lower mind and the lower spheres of life, it is free. Then it does not matter whether it has a physical body or not; it is free to function on any of the higher planes. We want you to establish firmly in your mind that you have within you now the capacity to expand your vision, your being, your activity, onto higher and wider planes of life.

We cannot describe the wonders of the invisible universe if you lack the capacity to imagine them. Imagination, or the power to imagine, is really the power of the Creator working in you. When you visualize, you create an image: but it can only express the measure in which God is present within you. The God-given power to see, to create, lies within every one of you; but only an infinitesimal part of the glory of God's creation is visible until you have unfolded and developed the necessary power of sight and imagination. You all have so much to hope for, to bring forth from your innermost self. The means of access to all the planes of life, from the physical to the dense etheric, the astral, the mental, the higher mental, and the celestial, and even beyond, is already within you; but you have to find the key and learn how to unlock the particular gate leading to them.

The earthly mind is the destroyer, the slayer of

truth. But a time will come when every soul will be aware of its own higher life and true self. Then it will be able to see the two selves in contrast—the limited earthly self and the eternal self which becomes stronger and more in evidence in everyday life. Then problems and difficulties no longer overwhelm a soul; they are kept in their place. The soul develops vision not only of God and heavenly things but sees earthly things in their true perspective as well. Such a soul's sensitivity enables him or her to penetrate the ethers and to receive radiation from the higher worlds.

One further point: the five-pointed star is a symbol of the awakening consciousness, of the dawn of light. It indicates that the light is dawning on those who seek. The six-pointed star, on the other hand, speaks of the soul that has found the light and reached a degree of equilibrium. It denotes an initiate, one who has attained balance, and has harmonized the extremes, the opposites, in life.

A MOMENT OF REFLECTION

Now, beloved brethren, reach out from the depths of your being. Open your soul wide, and in the very act of opening your mind and your heart to love, you become love and are in harmony with the Infinite. Love, infinite, universal, abundant love is that from which you came, and that which you are. And the whole purpose of life is that you shall realise this beauty and this love, and by continuing to express it, grow, grow, grow in the perfection of the God life which dwells within you and from which you were born.

III

KARMA AND REINCARNATION:
THE LONG JOURNEY

REMEMBER always that there are many different levels of consciousness in human kind. Not all people are at the same stage; when you look out into the world, even at your own friends and acquaintances, you can recognize what appear on the surface to be instances of great injustice. Some people seem to be blessed with many joys, both material and spiritual, while others, apparently equally deserving, are deprived of opportunities.

So you are forced to accept the truth that, on the surface at any rate, injustice and inequality exist. There is only one answer to the problem of why there seem to be injustice and inequality; it is that men and women are at different stages on a long journey. It is a journey which necessitates their constant return to physical conditions; because the soul only learns by experiencing life's limitations.

Ours is not the first nor the only voice to pronounce this truth; in the study of comparative religion you will come across it many times. A person returns to conditions in the physical world that he or she has previously created for him- or herself. Questions will immediately arise, such as, 'Why should I come back to such a state of life?' 'Why cannot I remember my past life?' 'Why should I have to suffer when I do not know why I am suffering?' 'How is it that I seem to be weak and unable to discipline or control myself and order my life better?' 'Why is it that my neighbour is strong and can do all the things I want to and cannot?'

These are questions that arise in the lower mind as soon as the angel comes to teach and awaken the soul to spiritual truth. Later on, we are going to speak about these angelic visitors, and the ministry of angels; but first we prepare the ground by reminding you all of the ancient law of reincarnation. Many today are so quickened and awakened that they know intuitively they have lived before; and they accept the fact that they have earned whatever problems or limitations face them—even in themselves, in their own character, as well as in the outer circumstances of their lives. The quickening of this sixth sense of intuition, or the inner light, which guides you to certain action and to certain lines of thought, is a great advance.

The question is often asked, for example: 'Why must the innocent so often suffer for the guilty?' We answer that the innocent do not suffer for the guilty. You only see from the standpoint of the earth and do not know the infinite love and mercy of your Creator. You fail to recognize the tender care that provides for those who suffer, those who are lonely and afraid. You see catastrophe, you see the dead body, the vacant house, and you exclaim, 'How terrible! How shocking is death!' But you do not know how Providence cares for those whose destiny it is to be suddenly released from the body in what may appear to be a terrible manner. For there is provision made. They themselves do not realize what is happening; they only know that they are living, moving, breathing in a world which seems identical with their former world, until with great tenderness and care they are brought to realize that they have left their old body, that they have 'died'. We in the spirit life watch these souls as they are awakening to this realization, and we know they feel intense joy and thankfulness that the crossing has been made so easily. That is their first reaction. They find they are living in a solid and real world, very like the world they have left behind but more beautiful. This tender love continually watches over a human being, not only at the time of death. It is always there, sustaining and enfolding each one. It always has been, it always will be.

Normally, when you pass out of the physical body after either a short or long life (depending on your karma) you come to a condition which some people call a state of purgatory. But this term is misleading; the condition is rather one of self-examination, of judgment *by yourself*, when you look into your own past and see the errors and mistakes that have been made.

Immediately a soul is released from the physical body and comes to our world, it starts a process of awakening. This may seem to you a contradiction because you have been told that for many a period of time elapses before they become aware of their new life. But remember that in our world there is no consciousness of time; thus a soul may apparently awaken immediately after death and yet by your time-measurement its period of quiescence may have been longer. This length of time is conditioned by the state of the man or woman at the time of passing on; but usually one who has been interested in spiritual truth quickly awakens to his or her new life. As soon as this happens, the lessons start, although the soul is not aware that it is learning lessons, any more than the average person on earth is aware that he or she is learning lessons and gradually evolving his or her own spiritual aspect.

One of the most usual methods of teaching is to take the soul to the Hall of Records, where it sees episodes in its life thrown on a cinema screen. Nothing is said to the soul; it just sees itself as it truly is.

It takes strength and courage to look into the mirror and to see yourself reflected, without camouflage; but accompanying this experience comes the teacher, in the guise of an acceptable friend who encourages and helps the one who is learning, in a gentle and beautiful way. The teacher neither condemns nor chides, but helps the pupil to understand that the pupil's life on earth is the result of former experiences.

You see, everything in the world of spirit is under the divine law of love. You are your own judge and your own punisher. The suffering you endure on earth and in spirit is unknowingly self-inflicted.

Even on earth if you do something that you know is foolish, the repercussion demonstrates to you how foolish you have been. Spiritual growth is based on the law of sowing and reaping. Yet we would stress the gentleness and love which governs the operation of this law.

Then, after that period of self-examination, which is tender and gentle, during which the soul is comforted and encouraged, there comes a period of rest and happiness, wherein the soul finds God. We cannot give a better description than to say that every part of the soul is satisfied for the time being. The soul is perfectly happy, seeing God everywhere and in everything.

This in turn stimulates the God within so that, having seen the glory of God, the soul wants to get back to work again—rather as after a long holiday you want again to be up and doing.

Karma and Opportunity

When the soul comes back to earth it carries a parcel with it, sometimes a very big one, which contains its karma. Its opportunities and capacity for spiritual unfoldment are limited by the size of the parcel. You talk loosely of paying off karma, but karma is very much more than a paying-off of debts incurred in a past life; it brings opportunity with it. The very act of paying off some karmic debt gives the soul a new chance to progress. This is why we say again and again: accept, accept your karma gratefully, cheerfully. It will seem hard; it is hard, because the lower bodies—which include the astral body of desire, the lower mental body—clamouring for their own way, rebel against the discipline karma imposes. But if you can not only accept what you dislike but realize the opportunity inherent in it, you will grow in consciousness. So the disciple must learn to accept his or her karma and use the opportunity it offers so as not to create more difficult karma. By a life of obedience to the brotherhood of life you will raise yourself until you become gentle and loving, true and wise, with all the virtues of a true Brother. This steady, earnest keeping-on-keeping-on, which may seem so dull but is so worthwhile, gets you there in the end.

With clearer vision, you will see how all human life works for harmony; that your karma operates all the time to develop a state of harmony in you and to free you from bondage by the earthly self, by the mind of earth. Karma is nothing to shrink from, but something to rejoice in, even if it is uncomfortable. All growth seems uncomfortable at the time. Birth too can be uncomfortable—but see what it leads to!

Now, what the individual experiences in the form of karma, opportunity and spiritual evolution is also taking place throughout the life of nations, in planets, in whole solar systems. All operate in obedience to one law of unfoldment and growth. We could almost describe it as a rhythmic in-breathing and out-breathing. Normally the process of breathing is so natural and harmonious that you are unaware of it. So also with the great rhythm of life. All the time the God-life is moving into human kind and withdrawing, coming into incarnation, passing out of it. Ages come and they sink away. They rise again. Life is one continual rhythm, a constant rhythmic movement towards perfection and still more perfection. Can perfection ever end? No; it is a scene that unfolds and unfolds to reveal ever more glorious vistas.

When you are able to go into the centre of your being, into the very heart of creation, into the centre of life, to the place of quietude and stillness of mind, emotions and body, deep within the centre of your being you realize the true way to act, to love. But the truths revealed to your spirit have to be translated into terms of the earth life.

We who come from that inner world are well aware of the practical details of human life. You may think that being spirit and disembodied, we are remote from the activities, pains and fears of our brother–sister on earth, but here you would be very much mistaken. The Brotherhood of the White Light are closely concerned with the evolution, happiness and wellbeing of all human kind. We have passed through many incarnations and can recall these human experiences when necessary. Therefore we can feel with you; we can understand your frustrations, limitations, anxieties and fears. We understand physical pain and spiritual suffering. We are part of you; we are one of you; we are with you, all of you.

But we love you; therefore we do not remove your problems and difficulties, for this would be neither kind nor good for you. We can only stand by your side and give you strength and love while you slowly learn by trial and error. As a result of your dealing with these difficulties, if you are moving on the clear path of light and open to the message being brought to you from the spirit, you will receive into your soul joy that would be lost to you if we were to remove your problems and difficulties. Only you, in companion-ship with God working in your heart, can experience the heavenly joy of learning those necessary truths. Each time your eyes are opened to the right way of life, each time you are able to touch the secret level of life, the light expands in your heart and soul, and life takes on a new aspect. You see with eyes both spiritual and physical a lovelier vista, a more profound beauty than you have ever seen before, and your heart sings with praise and thanksgiving to your Creator.

Let us give you a simple example of what we mean. It is said that a young man and woman truly in love see the world as something so much more beautiful than they did before. Love has quickened the spirit within them, and love, even in its lowliest form, has a magical power. It makes the lovers happy and reveals beauty to them.

We are trying, brethren, to bring you into the innermost centre of life and your own innermost centre, which is the basis of all action, the centre from which you will receive an answer to every problem.

The question is often asked, how can people be happy in the spirit world if they can see those they love unhappy on earth? The soul free from the bond-age of flesh and earthly limitations meets the loved one from earth during the latter's sleep. There is not the separation that you imagine. You are being trained to seek for the inner light, the life of spirit; you are being taught how to rise into a higher state of conscious life where you will meet your beloved in sleep, and both you and your loved one will rejoice at the reunion. Although the time comes when you have to return to your body, you do so knowing that you and the one you love are not separated, that he or she is living a natural and a happy life linked with your own. Souls are not drawn together in physical life unless there is a strong spiritual attraction. It is the attraction of karma; and although conditions between the two may sometimes be difficult, any lack of understanding is the result of karma that has to be worked out. It is no use kicking against the pricks. The only way to deal with such a situation is to face it out and ask yourself: 'What would the Master do?' Look within and see where your fault lies, as well as the fault of the one with whom you are at variance. This applies to you all, and it offers a solution for all ills and all disagreements and the unhappiness brought about through conflict between personalities.

Again, we want you to understand that your life here is interwoven with your life in the spirit. As you are on earth, so you are here in the world of spirit, the world in which your guides and loved friends live. They come close to help you, to lift you up when you are in despair. And incidentally, when you open yourself to receive this blessing it brings new life to the physical body. People grow old because of the emotions, the anxieties, the worries they permit themselves; they grow sick through stress and strain. If you always remained attuned to the Great White Light you would not suffer disease.

The soul in incarnation suffers limitations and enjoys opportunities earned in the past; and it will be born into circumstances where it will have the best opportunities to achieve the greatest good, to make the greatest progress.

The human mind misconstrues the mercy and goodness of God and thinks of karma as being bad. Karma is rather an opportunity to learn, presented to you as the result of your past thought, speech and action.

We cannot do your work; neither can the brother or sister by your side give your particular service to life, for you all have your own contribution to make to the whole of God's creation. You are builders, co-workers with the Creator. Whatever your job, do it to the very best of your ability. Should you find yourself frustrated, limited, you can surely liberate yourself by divine law, and this applies to every aspect of your life—to health, domestic conditions, material or mental states. All these can be recreated by your remaining true to the spirit of Christ within and around you.

God bless you all. You do not walk alone, for your guardian angel is helping you in every endeavour.

A MOMENT OF REFLECTION

Let us now visualize the Sun, the centre of your solar system, the spiritual Sun invisible behind the physical sun, and the spiritual rays descending upon humanity, working in the most beautiful and wonderful way to get through into your consciousness the divine glory of your true being . . . rays working, blending, harmonizing. No matter what apparent disruption occurs on the physical plane, the rays are permeating, drawing together the threads, and weaving a glorious rainbow of colour and beauty throughout creation. Ultimately the colour and beauty resolves itself back again into that perfect light, the White Spirit, the Great White Light. There is no such thing as chance, no such thing as accident——everything working in perfect law, under the direction of the great spirits at the head of the rays which permeate humanity.

IV

DUAL SOULS

NOW WE TOUCH on a rather delicate subject, that of 'dual souls'. Some believe there is no such thing as twin souls; others believe that everyone has a counterpart and that some day both will come together. We would say first of all that you are not intended to look for your twin soul on earth, and abandon your karmic responsibilities with your existing partner simply because you have found someone you think is your affinity. As a general principle, you must realize that you have been placed in a certain position in life with karmic responsibilities as well as opportunities. The whole object of your being here is that you may grow spiritually. To grow spiritually you must honour your responsibilities and the debts you owe to your companions.

Nevertheless it is true that there are two aspects of the perfect soul, the female and the male. For purposes of spiritual evolution, these opposites separate in order to gain experience in earth life. Eventually, having earned the right to happiness, they are allowed to meet. They come together, usually but not always, after death. Sometimes, when the conditions are right and the soul has attained a degree of spirituality that permits it, these two live for a period in a state of perfect happiness in the spirit life.

In that world, souls can find themselves in a new environment, which is often the etheric counterpart of the planet Venus. It is not unnatural that dual souls are drawn to this planet of perfect love: not physical passion, but pure love, perfect companionship, perfect harmony. Here the two blend as one, though the two can always, by mutual consent, separate when the need arises. In reality, however, once union has been made in full consciousness, there can never again be separation. In perfect love there *is* no separation.

The Means to reach Heaven

God has put in your heart the means to reach Heaven, the key to things supernal. This dark earth cannot hold you. If the atmosphere today is thick with fog, the fog is only something that human kind has created, not God. But if you live all the time thinking of sunshine and the glorious Sun of God, so that your mind is filled with light, then for you the darkness and fog will recede. You will be lanterns, all alight; and as soon as there are enough lights the fogs and mists will disappear.

Jesus said, *I AM the light of the world*. How do you interpret this? Jesus cannot have meant that he was really a light, say, on a dark night? But he did mean that the 'I AM', the Christ within is the light, the resurrection and the life. The 'I AM' within each being throws a light out from the heart which penetrates all mists and darkness.

You talk about 'living in the light'. When you are in a spiritual place you really feel you are in the light. You close your eyes and meditate on spiritual sunlight; you see radiant beings clothed in all the colours of the spectrum; you wander in your meditations in gardens of indescribable beauty; you meet people with shining faces, who are all love and wisdom; then you come back to what you call reality. But it is the vision you enjoyed when meditating that was real; for that

*John 8 : 12

is your true life, the life of the spirit. What you come back to is illusion. Do you realize that your physical world is illusory? That it is in reality built of light? That your physical body, if you could see it with clear vision, is composed of light?

We are trying to explain that there is a perpetual interpenetration of life from above to below. All life is one; but you, a spark of God, a child of God, have to learn this by undergoing experience in the densest form of manifestation on the earth. Remember, you were created to become master of matter. Yet even at the physical level you are still part of your Creator, still a son or daughter of God. All creation—natural, animal, human, angelic—all forms of life are of the one spirit and all are one great family with God their Father and the Divine Mother. This mystical truth is expressed in the Holy Trinity and symbolized by the triangle. The last principle we gave to the White Eagle Lodge* is that the goal of human life is the re-union with the Holy Family, or the blessed Trinity of Father, Mother and Child. In other words, the spark of life breathed forth from the heart of the Creator travels far to incarnate in earth, it gains wisdom and

*The White Eagle Lodge was founded under White Eagle's direction in 1936. For more details, see the introduction.

understanding, and eventually returns with a full consciousness of itself as part of God.

This is the goal of every human soul. Think of what lies before you. Do not be discouraged. Do not weary of well-doing. Do not lay down your tools until you have completed your task.

We want to bring home to you the realization of the divine law of love; a belief in the great spirit family; a belief in the angels; a belief in the vast spiritual universe around you in which this planet has crystallized into a form of matter you can see and understand. Do not limit your thoughts and your conception of life to this. Let your thoughts go forth into a spiritual universe, into an outer space beyond and far beyond your little planet; mingle with your brethren of other worlds.

It is the purpose of life that we should expand in consciousness. Life itself is consciousness. We would again emphasize the age-old truth that all knowledge is within you; the whole universe resides in the life-spark in your heart centre. You seek outside yourself; it is a natural instinct to look out and reach up for knowledge. But there comes a time when the growing consciousness in you reveals the profound truth that all knowledge is within yourself. From within yourself you will receive the eternal wisdom.

It is not solely for the purpose of helping you to unfold the powers of the soul that we say meditation is the way. It is because only thus will you find God and the truth of life. 'Man, know thyself; and thou shalt know God and the universe' were the words engraved over the entrance to the ancient Mystery Schools.

You often read or hear that a man or woman contains all knowledge within him- or herself, but you do not fully appreciate the meaning of this. The sages or elder brethren withdraw from the physical world and outer mental plane for long periods. While in meditation in the silent places, they dwell in the consciousness of all life; they enter into the lifestreams; they are aware of the penetration of the vibrations of the cosmos into their soul; they become fully conscious of their origin and of their completion. They are then at one with God in Whom is all wisdom, all knowledge; and because they are with God they can influence and direct human kind towards the Supreme Consciousness.

Think about the soul-emanations from these great people. Try to imagine the countless threads or projections of light that constantly go forth, penetrating all life, your own included. Some of you may doubt that such a great being could ever be in tune with your soul. But we can assure you that this work is going on constantly at a certain level of conscious life. The mission of these great ones is to enlighten all souls who are praying and ready. You yourself by aspiration and goodness in thought and life can contact them. Nothing hinders you unless you debar yourself by breaking the spiritual law, which is love.

We are trying to show you that all knowledge is already within you; that the life within you is conscious of everything. You are learning in incarnation to expand your consciousness, and with this expansion of consciousness comes all knowledge.

One supreme factor helps you along your path: your innate urge to grow. Just as the seed in the ground puts forth its roots and struggles upward through the dark soil to the light, so also human kind works. At first, people work unconsciously; they do not know what they are doing. Nevertheless, consciously or unconsciously they reach ceaselessly towards an expansion of consciousness. In the course of this effort for self-expression and growth they do some very queer things. They become full of egotism and intolerance, always pushing others out of their way. Having seen one tiny aspect of truth, a person thinks he or she is the only one who has ever found it. If the person by his or her side sees another aspect of truth, they quarrel with one another and say: 'What you've got isn't truth at all. Mine is the only truth!' In every phase of life the person makes the assertion that he or she is better than all others. But at last, when the soul begins to recognize and meditate on God, his or her expansion of consciousness becomes harmonious; he or she begins to see not one aspect only, but all truth.

We have said that one power is ever-present to help you in your growth, your innate urge upward. In a sense this power is drawing us to itself like a tremendous magnet. Remember also that throughout time the Creator has sent messengers to earth. The Creator has sent the Son made in His own image, the image in which you, too, are created. You can only understand, love and look up to someone like yourself. This is why the Son has come to human kind in different guises, throughout the ages. At Christmas particularly, and at the great Sun festivals, a power radiates over the earth from the Son: a power that stimulates this urge in humanity to reach upward and grow.

A MOMENT OF REFLECTION

We would draw your attention to the Christ Circle in the heavens above earth. Is it really above earth? It seems to be; but in reality it encircles and enfolds earth, and from its centre there shines a great cosmic jewel. Think for a moment about the heavenly being this jewel represents and about the hierarchies surrounding this being: all radiating love, life, beauty, truth to earth; ever drawing you upwards to the fuller, more perfect life. Your earthly mind makes it difficult for you to believe what we say, but in meditation you will feel the radiation and wonder of that influence.

V

LOVE IS THE BRIDGE

CAN YOU define love? When we think of love, we at once feel an outflowing, a giving, to you, to all life. To love means to give. When you love you seem to go outwards, flow out in order to help, to serve. But as you cannot breathe out without breathing in, so you cannot give love without receiving. Love is an out-breathing and an in-breathing. It is a light that burns deep within; a warmth, a certainty, an inner knowing. Whenever you are not acting, speaking or thinking in love, you are unhappy because you are out of harmony. The earthly mind will not usually admit this. It goes to extremes to justify itself, but the inner you knows that you are out of harmony when you are not feeling this emotion of love. Love is God; and God is discovered within the heart. If love is absent you flounder about and cannot understand the meaning of God, and God remains a mystery.

The divine essence that is love is God, is the Creator. God is love, and all life and all form is created by love, on whatever level love operates. Let us say here that form is not only created on the physical plane, but on other levels of life. Is it possible that form can be created in the spirit world? Most certainly. Is a woman to be denied the joy of motherhood in the spirit world? Why should she be? As below, so above; as above, so below. If she longs to hold her babe in her arms, that joy awaits her in the spirit life.

Each one of you is accompanied by an illumined soul from the world of light—a guide, companion or teacher—and certainly by the one who is the affinity of your spirit, for where love is there is no separation. So, my children, if your particular loved companion is in spirit life, try to realize that the etheric bridge can be crossed, for truly angels and your loved ones can come to you once you have raised your consciousness to them.

Try to realize this truth within yourself; to realize that you can create the bridge by love, by your belief in God's love, by your belief in love itself. When doubts assail you, remember that they are only the promptings of your lower mind, or what you are sometimes pleased to call 'reason.' It is only this lower, material self that cuts you off from those you love who live in the land of light.

This message is specially for those who feel the need of comfort, who want reassurance of the continued companionship of a loved one, for we can see many troubled hearts; we can see loneliness and in some cases almost a despairing spirit. We would not materialize the spiritual life, or try to give you proof to satisfy your physical senses. But we pray that we may raise you to that level where you may become aware of the life of spirit.

There are people who declare it impossible for those in Heaven to reach those on earth, saying that those in a heavenly state are forever cut off from earthly life. But they are only cut off if you yourselves do the cutting. If you are unfolding your spiritual life, you will naturally rise heavenward and those in heaven will come halfway to meet you. It is the Creator's will that the sons and daughters of God should learn to penetrate the heavy mists surrounding them on earth, mists of selfishness and materialism which obscure the heavenly world.

The lower self holds you down to physical matter. But by right living and right thinking, by aspiration and even by the way of crucifixion, you can find your way to the heavenly state. Once there, you find truth. You find truth through love. It may be through love of nature, love of beauty, love of music, love of another human being, love of God; but your love for God will be the same as your love for humanity, because you will find and love your God in human kind.

You see how desirable it is to develop a quality that will enable you to look above the crowds in the market place and see the master or hear his or her voice? Open your eyes and look, and you will surely find the one you long to hear and to see. All prejudice in yourself must be broken down first. How can this be done? In one way only: by filling the heart with love. And what does love mean? Love means 'thinking good'. Many qualities and emotions are mistaken for love, but love is simply the longing of the lover to make the loved one supremely happy. At the human level of true love, any thought for self is overruled by thoughtfulness for the object of that love. In a broader and wider sense, love in the soul means that the soul is longing above all to give love and happiness.

Now when a person lives and works, as we hope you are all striving to do, to bless every creature, to do his or her best always with hand and heart; when a person is living so that he or she is truly giving out love to life on every level, then that person is drawing very close to liberation, to mastership. All the reforms that you long for will come through your effort towards God. This you won't believe—but do think it over. It is what you do, what you think, what you say, that matters.

The saints of all time, not only of yesterday but of today, have all attained a degree of spiritual life wherein they not only comprehend love, but their whole being is love expressed in service—to life itself, to the universe as a whole. The saint, through love, has attained mastery over him- or herself, over the forces or the invisible rays that are continually playing upon life.

The whole universe is full of these invisible rays, vibrations of power. They may be used to build, to construct, or else they may be used to break down and destroy. If they are constructive in nature, you refer to them as 'good'; but if they break down and destroy, you say 'evil'. By the power that comes from love, a master can manipulate or direct those rays for good, to bring about equilibrium, to hold the balance. Have you ever thought of the vital necessity of holding this balance? Whenever the balance is not held, even in your material world, there is chaos.

Let us feel our close communion with our elder brethren. They want you continually to remind yourself that you are divine, you are spirit. Cultivate your inner, your spiritual life, and do not neglect any kind action that will serve your companions or bring them happiness.

The True Personality

Some say you must get beyond personality; but they do not understand what personality means. St John said, *he that loveth not his brother whom he hath seen, how can he love God whom he hath not seen?** In everyone, in their personality, is the spirit of God, albeit often closely veiled. Jesus, who was all compassion, showed how to find this God in human kind. He looked into the soul of those who drew close to him; he saw their whole life, and the burden of their karma. He was compassionate and forgave much.

When you hear it said that you must get beyond personality, it means that the spirit within must develop and grow strong, so that you are not deceived by

**I John : 4*

appearances, or bound down by personal things. To get beyond personality is to be released from its bondage. But at the same time remember the value of personality. Through the personality of Jesus the Christ, the divine human being is presented to you, and this helps you draw nearer to an understanding of that Divine Spirit. The picture presented to you of Jesus as a loving, tender saviour conveys the essence of the love of the perfect being, and as you contemplate this loving personality your soul reaches up towards the embrace and blessing of the divine love that is the saving grace of human kind. For when you see the divinity of Christ revealed, you become at one with the divine spirit. It comes into you; it goes forth from you.

Jesus expressed this truth in few words. He said, *I am in the Father, and the Father in me. If ye had known me, ye should have known my Father also.**

Do you now see the value of a personality, beautified, perfected by the divine spirit? Then imagine all humanity manifesting this same spirit of love. Why, this would be universal brotherhood, it would extend to the animal level, to all nature, even to the gems in the earth! The very stones would cry out.

But before human kind can rise from the grave of

*John 14 : 11, 7

earthiness, before humanity can return to the Father, all pass through an initiation called crucifixion. The crucifixion of Jesus was a physical demonstration of spiritual truth, of the soul's struggle to release itself from the bondage of earth.

You have all suffered, and you know in how many different ways each human can be crucified. You see, it comes not only once; life seems for some a continual crucifixion, continual pain and suffering, and a wrestling all the time to get beyond, get above, the pain which is the lot of physical man and woman. The crucifixion has to be enacted many, many times until there comes a time, as it came to Jesus, when the suffering of the body is real only to the onlookers. The soul is no longer there, it is beyond the suffering of the body.

In the biblical apocrypha you can read how Jesus was talking with his disciples even while his body was being crucified. He himself was free; he was no longer with the body or even conscious of its suffering, because he had attained mastery over it. This is important for you to grasp; because when you have to undergo crucifixion during your fight with the lower self, the real you, the true child of God, can stand above and apart from it. People may say, 'How terrible it is to see such suffering!' That is right; you must always feel love and sympathy. But the sage says, 'A wise man grieves neither for the living nor for the dead'. A wise person has passed beyond, knowing that the soul is in the hands of God, pursuing its appointed path; that out of suffering, out of crucifixion, comes the resurrection. This we would impress on you, that after periods of pain and suffering, which you must accept resolutely, comes new life, rebirth.

A MOMENT OF REFLECTION

The saints who have attained all gather round you now. There is neither past nor future. All is now. All are with you. The spirit of Jesus is close, and as you make this companionship real in your heart, so you will perceive his form on a higher level of manifestation; but it will be the real and perfect form of the Master Jesus. In the same way, through your soul-effort and the spiritual power from God, you can create the form of any saint. It won't be just fantasy; it will be the real being, because that being is at-one, is a part of God, and you too are part of God. This is what may be called a state of cosmic consciousness, when all are one and you are with all. All you have ever known, loved and admired will be with you then, for in love there is no separation.

VI

QUALITIES TO DEVELOP

YOU ARE IN the human body for a twofold purpose; first to find the glory of God both in yourself and in all life, and secondly to discover through incarnation those spiritual truths through which you will achieve infinite happiness.

The law is that you shall love God with all your heart and soul and mind, and in doing so you will naturally love your neighbour because God is *in* your neighbour. Life is one whole. You cannot become isolated from God or your neighbour, and the tendency in all life is towards unification. First comes the development and the growth of the individual and the God-consciousness in the individual, and next the unification in full consciousness with the whole of life. You know then that you cannot hurt any living thing without hurting yourself, the whole of life; and that every kind and tender act comes back to you in blessing.

You are living in an age, my children, when the rate of humanity's spiritual unfoldment is being speeded up. The suffering of two world wars has hastened the process; and as a result, human kind, through the mind and through the development of science, is searching for truth.

Humility

Simplicity should be the prayer of every aspirant; because only when the soul becomes truly humble can it be receptive to the guidance and love of the invisible brethren and the angelic messengers who wait under God's command to come to you and to all human beings. The key that unlocks the door to these heavenly mysteries lies not in the human mind but in the heart. Truth is simple, but because it is so simple it is hidden from powerful intellects, or those who play with words; yet it is revealed to the loving heart.

Do not mistake us. We do not suggest that men and women of learning cannot receive this heavenly blessing, guidance and inspiration. We refer to those who are arrogant mentally, those blinded by their arrogance and who have yet to undergo an initiation or experience which through pain or joy (pain and joy are but reflections of each other) brings humility.

Each soul must go through such experiences, perhaps many times, before understanding what it means to be humble. The greatest mind is ever the humble mind; you will find this in all elder and wise brethren. Humility is indeed the most important virtue if the soul is to attain any degree of understanding and experience of God. Through the experience of human life with all its pain and joy, the soul is quickened and enabled to see truth—which means of course that it can recognize its relationship with the Eternal Spirit.

Patience

Now patience is needed in this gradual journey towards unfoldment. You cannot jump over obstacles, as many people try to do. The ancient mystery teaching says that no candidate for initiation must try to rush forward. It is the lower self that wants to rush forward and get to the destination quickly. As soon as people awaken and consciously tread the spiritual path, they desire to know more and more. The mind becomes greedy for knowledge. This must be curbed. There must be self-discipline and tranquillity. Tranquillity is of the utmost importance, because the soul is only receptive to the ministry of angels in its tranquil moments. Many, many times the guardian angel draws close to the soul entrusted to its care; but when the soul is so concerned with the world and with itself it cannot receive the guidance.

So, if you would comprehend spiritual truth and divine law, you must follow your inner light; you must not only obey the voice of God within you but trust it; and even if you sometimes feel restive under the experiences which come to you, you must keep faith. You need faith in and obedience to the voice of God within; you need faith in that divine guiding light which is working through you. When you have achieved these virtues, you no longer question with your earthly mind the wisdom of God's laws. You surrender to the love of God, and you accept, accept, accept.

Against this, the earthly mind will pop up again and say, 'But surely I should accept nothing against the reason that God, if there be a God, has given me'. How true! But the real reasoning power in you can always be satisfied by spiritual light. When light dawns in your heart, when through your own experience you have been drawn close to the heart of God or the Master, you both see and know. You do not then need books to tell you, nor yet anyone speaking as we are speaking to you. Your very experience in meditation, or in a state of contemplation or prayer, gives you something that can never be described; but in this experience, which is communion with your Creator, with God, you know truth.

If you are going on a journey to a distant country, usually you will make some effort to find out as much as you can about it. You will probably obtain maps and guidebooks, which will help you by giving directions on how to get there and by describing the country to which you are going. Beyond that they can do nothing. They cannot provide you with the means of transport; they cannot travel for you. You have actually to travel, to experience for yourself, and thus learn so much more than you can ever learn from maps and guidebooks. We are trying to make plain that when you are quickened in spirit, knowing that you have come from afar and are embarked on a long journey, then you are ready to experience all the beauty laid out before and all around you. You can experience the joy of your physical state and can breathe in the divine life forces in fuller consciousness.

You must experience every detail of life with all your senses, physical, mental and spiritual.

Harmony

From time to time we stress the need for harmony, but by 'living in harmony' we do not mean remaining unaware of things which need to be righted; rather we mean training yourself to do everything that seems necessary in the most harmonious way. Many times we have said, 'Always work for harmony', not only because the harmonious life is so much easier and happier, but because harmony is the very keynote of the universe.

There is controversy as to whether nations and individuals should threaten each other with weapons of destruction in order to preserve law and order. Some say it is not right to be unarmed and without the means of protection; others that it is wrong to consider the use of what are called nuclear weapons or even to test them. Many of you may feel puzzled as to what is the right thing to do.

Now we do not enter into earthly or political arguments about it, for this is not our way. But we can tell you what the White Brothers would do. Is it right, you will say, to sit down passively and not fight evil?

St Paul said, *Overcome evil with good.** You will say, 'That is impossible; we must do something'. Some feel strongly on the subject of the protection of the weaker; it is the natural instinct for you to protect your loved ones and friends and to preserve the peace of your life. And yet, you know, there is a divine law, and God is your protector. But you must yourself be the channel through which God can work. This means that the one who understands spiritual law should be active in using that law, spreading the knowledge of that law among others. In other words, through you God helps humanity to a better state of life. This is quite different from what you loosely call pacifism. It is an active, not a passive state. You can be a channel for good. You can strive to be good. You can strive to act on the square in your daily life. You can abhor untruthfulness, deception, unkindness. You can abhor killing in any form. You can be an active channel for the divine creative power to reach humanity, to help humanity to awaken to the true way of life.

*Romans 12 : 21

Dealing with Increased Sensitivity

But there is a great deal for you to overcome. For instance, as you progress on the spiritual path, you are also increasing your sensitivity; the nervous system becomes very sensitive. It is like walking on a razor's edge, because on the one hand you need to develop the sensitivity that enables you to receive heavenly guidance, comfort and help in your daily life; and on the other you have to develop the inner power of God, which brings tranquillity. The power of God is love. The soul that has developed true love acquires wisdom. The soul that develops tranquillity achieves the quality of God's peace. When the soul can reach the degree of tranquillity that brings humility, its eyes are opened and it sees far beyond the limitations of the ordinary physical mind.

Now one of the greatest helps to you on your journey in search of God (and this is the purpose of your life) is meditation. Books will not get you there, although they can point the way; words will not take you. You have to make the journey yourself. You have to experience for yourself those higher states of consciousness, the reality of the inner world. This can begin for you in the practice of meditation. On your first contact with the universal life, through meditation, something happens which has never happened before.

Maybe in your early experiences of meditation, you have been disappointed and felt that you were getting nowhere; you saw nothing; you heard nothing. Perhaps it just seemed as though you were sitting in darkness—but not quite, because occasionally you may have seen or imagined a colour; or you may have imagined something but you could not trust yourself. You might have said, 'I don't think it was true; it was in my mind'. But what you have to remember, is that spiritual truth and awareness is the greatest gift of God to human kind, and so this gift has to be patiently sought. If it were easy to find that state of indescribable joy, all the world would be there too.

Life after death, or your meeting with or relationship with God, depends entirely on your soul's consciousness. You can always be completely alone with God. Think of this—you and your God … alone.

We are talking like this because there are so many people today searching for truth, longing to know if there be a God at all, or if there is really any life beyond this troubled earth. We are endeavouring to give human kind the simple truth, and point the way to God.

But you must tread the path yourself and this means not only effort in weekly or possibly daily meditation, although this is of vital importance; it also means effort in living your daily life—and this is not easy. We know the problems of physical life because we have ourselves lived it, and this is perhaps the reason why a discarnate spirit is permitted to speak to you thus.

You tend to think of the spirit life as being life after death. But you are always living in a world of spirit; you are living now in a world of spirit, but you don't know it. You are like blindfolded men and women in a beautiful country. Few of you ever catch a glimpse of the beauty. You who catch these glimpses are learning how to release yourselves from darkness. During times of true and pure meditation you are released into the world of spirit. When you finally leave the body, when you have finished with this dress for a time, you move on in the soul world.

The whole purpose of life is the growth of this consciousness. Until you are conscious of yourself in this world, you are not really living; and until you are conscious of the God within you, you cannot expand to become aware of the Eternal Now.

When you meditate, you may perhaps see, you may hear described by the leader of your group, the substance of which buildings on the astral plane are made. It will appear as pulsating light; the impression you receive as you enter these buildings is of radiant light. But the light never hurts your eyes, for you are adjusted to it and it adjusts itself to you. You see and register only what you are capable of seeing and registering, no more. But in the substance of the buildings, colour is always noticed. A highly-developed sensitive will register many lovely colours, all born from the seven primary colours and the seven rays used by the Elohim, the Silent Watchers, Great Ones, each at the head of his or her own particular ray. Above all, we want to give you the picture of the Sun and of these rays of colour born from it.

Every soul in incarnation is affected all the time by planetary influences which play upon human life through the chakras.* Each chakra is linked with its planet and with the colour associated with that planet. Thus, in healing, a group is guided to use mentally certain rays of colour to bring harmony into the human body; to restore what is lacking. All need

* *The chakras, or 'psychic centres', are sensitive points in the etheric body, connected with the nervous system, roughly corresponding in position with the ductless glands in the physical body, through which contact with higher and finer spheres of consciousness is established.*

healing in one form or another, for none is perfect yet. To you the physical symptom is the first sign of the disease; but it is the general vibration, the harmony of the individual, that is first disturbed, and this is the cause of the physical disorder. The instruments of an orchestra must be exactly attuned if the music is to be harmonious and perfect. So also with the bodies of men and women.

In passing, we would say that music heals. Even when not quite to your taste, it can be used by the angels to heal, to create, or perhaps to break down what is unwanted. Every colour of the spectrum, every planet, has its own particular tone on which it vibrates and to which the individual in turn responds. We often bid you to 'breathe in the light.' In doing so you breathe in harmony, healing, for all the colours are contained in the white light.

We hope we have given you a picture of the linking-up of your own personality and your own heart, which is the Sun of your universe, with the greater Sun and the greater Universe. When you think of the intermingling of all these spheres of life, and of the rays from the first great Cause shining through them all, you will understand why you can be helped by striving always to create harmony both in yourself and in your surroundings. On you will depend the harmony and beauty of your environment. You should be expressing God; all your surroundings should be beautiful—not necessarily rich and sumptuous, but simple, clean, orderly, beautiful; nothing should be out of place in God's world. So part of the process of spiritual training and development is to obey Divine Law in your mind—to let your mind be orderly and harmonious. Thus the harmony of the spheres will impress itself on your soul and you will live in the consciousness of divine harmony, perfection, summed up in one word—love.

Angelic Assistance

Now we have spoken to you of the ministry of angels and how you can best open your awareness of their guidance. An angel is a messenger from heavenly spheres. Angels are God's messengers sent to help human souls through spiritual experiences. Certain grave and important events in your life are always attended by angels. We were saying a moment or two ago that we were permitted to speak to you through the instrument of another physical body, because we ourselves have lived in a physical body, and we retain memories of it; we retain memories of the suffering, the difficulties and the heartaches and so we are able to help you. But guardian angels, heavenly visitors, do not function at the same level or in the same way as human beings, even though they come into close contact with them.

Some of you have queer things happen to you, and you say, 'What an extraordinary thing! By chance I went somewhere and….' or 'by chance I picked up a book and….' or 'by chance someone spoke to me'. These simple happenings, ones that have brought an enormous change into your life, do not come by chance, but as the result of guidance by your guardian angel. We suggest that each one of you has not only a human companion or guide in the unseen world, but also a guardian angel who comes from supernal states, and has you in his or her care.

Of course you have been given freewill. Every time you respond to a higher, a good, a spiritual impulse, you are helped by your guardian angel. No effort that you make to reach high, to respond to that higher influence, is ever wasted. But according to the degree to which the soul responds to heavenly influences and thereby advances on the path, it will also be beset with human problems; human relationships will press upon it. You can respond to them guided either by the higher spiritual impulse, or by the instincts of the lower self. That pure light from heaven can help you be kind, tolerant, patient and faithful—all the qualities that the soul needs in order to become in time the perfect son or daughter of God; but it must be by your own decision, your own freewill.

We want you to recognize these two aspects—on the one hand, angelic guidance, angelic help; and on the other, human guidance, human help. It lies with you to accept or reject them both. The guardian angel helps the soul when it desires to be helped.

We would like to add that the guardian angel is always present at the time of birth, as also is the form, the influence, if you like that word better, of Divine Mother. The guardian angel always cares for the soul coming into incarnation, and the Divine Mother's love helps the physical birth.

When you listen to music, you are perhaps unaware of what is being created. You love harmony; you enjoy music and rhythm with your mind, and indeed with your heart. It does something to your being. But few people understand the real influence of music. When you listen to music, remember that it is drawing to you angels who have a work to do with the evolution of human kind. Angels are also drawn close when ritual is exactly performed. A great power is wielded by the angels of ritual; it calls them and they bring with them a heavenly power. We are speaking of course of pure, white ritual. Similarly, at a marriage ceremony, when there is true spiritual aspiration and correct and spiritual ritual is performed (which of course takes place in the soul as well as on the outer plane) angels draw near.

Lastly, the moment comes when you have to 'die', as you call it. But of course you never die; the spirit and the soul which clothes it is gently withdrawn and passes upward through the head. The physical body is left like an empty shell, but the arisen soul is received into the heavenly state. The angel of death is present at every passing, no matter how it happens. The soul is caught up by the angel and is gently borne into the world of light. Usually the soul is in the form of a babe. The passing from the physical state to the next state is the same as birth into this physical life; the soul seems to become as a baby child. The little form is built up above the physical body and is enfolded in the love of the angel of death. It is wrapped in the loving robe of the angel of death and borne away to its new state of life, where other angels wait to minister to it and gradually awaken it to a state of awareness of its new life.

We would like you to understand that all life is held in God's love, and preparation is made for all the important events in your life. We would have you think of the Great White Spirit as One who ever loves you. Remember, my children, that God, your Father Mother God, will never, never forsake you. You are held closely in His–Her love. God's ministering angels will help you. Ask, seek and you will receive spiritual and physical blessings in full measure. This is divine law.

A MOMENT OF REFLECTION

We raise you from the confused turmoil and clamour of the physical life into the consciousness of God and God's angels. Let us then rise in spirit and enter the temple of prayer; and in unison with all brethren of the same heart we pray to our Father–Mother God. O gracious Spirit, we pray to become attuned to Thy love. . . .

Humbly giving thanks for all the blessings of life, we ask that the light of Christ, Thy Son, may shed its rays all

over the earth and be received into humble hearts everywhere.
We leave you the spirit of tranquillity, of inner peace
and a feeling of deep thankfulness that God is; and that you
are safe in Divine Love; for has not God given the angels
charge over you to keep you in all your ways?

Amen.

VII

CLEAR SIGHT

MANY PEOPLE think that only a few can have clear vision, see clairvoyantly. True, there may be only a few at the present time, but what one can do, all may do. If only one person has the gift of vision it means that the same gift lies latent in all people, for all are sons and daughters of God. Did not Jesus the Christ say: *He that believeth on me, the works that I do shall he do also; and greater works than these shall he do**? But whether or not the gift becomes effective is a matter of karma.

Now we will try to show you the meaning of clairvoyance, or clear sight. Many of you may have a degree of clairvoyance, or may think you have. We remind you that the degrees of clear sight and understanding can range from the lowest to an immense range of heights in the heavenly life. You may have a degree of clairvoyance on the lower astral, the plane just beyond the

**John 14 : 12*

physical; or you may have clear vision of the cosmos. Between those two there are many levels. Clairvoyance does not mean only the seeing of forms. Clairvoyance also means clear perception, clear vision of truth, clear vision of a future life on earth, a vision of what might be if all people acted from the heart of life.

The seven rays of the spectrum are all contained in the one white ray, which we will call the Christ Light. The Christ Light contains all the rays, each creative, each having the power to affect all forms of matter. All these rays proceed from the centre or heart of the universe, which is the continual beat of *love, love, love*—a giving out, an outpouring of healing, an ever-creative power. These are the rays that cause the musician to create, to hear his or her music and to record it; the rays that inspire the mind of the writer, or stimulate the vision of the artist.

All creative work proceeds from the centre or heart of both the spiritual and physical universes. The impulse going forth acts upon the human mind, causing a person to imagine. This is your term for it, imagination. All creative artists use the gift of ideation or imagination. These people are each in their particular way developing, unfolding their degree of clairvoyance, or clairaudience.

We say this to help you understand the gift of clairvoyance and to work within your own temple, within your heart, from that centre which is the Christ atom, the Christ seed—or the jewel within the lotus. From that centre, you may proceed in your work of ideation, imagination, responding to the vibrations of the invisible world around you, and from your own Christ power within rebuilding your mental field, your health field, your physical and material surroundings.

All form is first created in the mind; and the human mind can be directed or manipulated by the mind and the power of God. Try to understand what we endeavour to teach, because it is so important to you as individuals. This creative gift is either making or breaking you. It can make your life a thing of joy and beauty or it can make it chaotic.

Good Thought

We want to impress on you the importance of right and good thought, of continual thoughts of goodwill. If this power of God-thought is strong in humanity and people pray earnestly for the establishment of goodwill and harmony on earth, then so much more help goes to those arranging and planning the future of human kind. We are able to tell you that the light has already broken into dark places and a clearer understanding is coming. Humanity has gained a great deal of knowledge and has absorbed the light of the Christ spirit through pain and loss. We see a better spirit coming among the people; but there is still a great deal to be done before humanity comes through the dark clouds of ignorance into the light. We see in the future that wars between nations will cease. We see the dawn of an entirely new way of life, such a state as you could not conceive at the present time.

Remember that the social and industrial problems of earth are only solved when love so fills the consciousness of human kind that a person puts first not his or her own good but that of his or her companions. All human kind must live in the one spirit, the one spirit of love, the spirit of Christ. This can only come about by sustained effort both on the earth plane and on other planes of existence; by continual effort to be as God created and wills us to be, sons and daughters of the Light. This spirit of brotherhood is slowly but definitely arising.

Thought creates. Your thought of today is externalized tomorrow. You think of war and disaster, and when the thought is strong enough these things actually manifest on the physical plane. What you think you become. What the world thinks today, it becomes tomorrow. Whatever you experience on earth lies first in the thought world. So also with life after death: when you leave your body you find yourself in a world of strong desires and passions if you have lived and thought in that way on earth. But the man or woman whose thoughts are kind, loving and simply good, who lives (according to his or her development and understanding of spiritual truth) to manifest the spirit of Christ, will awaken in that very world of thought that he or she has created. On earth you can hide your thoughts; but in the spirit world you can no longer do this. All that you have been thinking is externalized in your spirit life. When you leave your physical body you can pass into a new world of great beauty and happiness, and only you can bar yourself from it.

At the same time, remember that the Divine Law is all love, and that a path of progress lies before every soul; every soul has the opportunity to grow in spirit and to give service. If a soul at first finds itself in an unpleasant condition it immediately has the opportunity to change, and it can quickly progress from limitation or 'purgatory' to a fuller life, and can very quickly rise above limitation into the third sphere of harmony and happiness.

As you think, as you imagine, so you become. The action of negative thought or imagination on a certain centre of the brain brings disease, lack of ease, lack of harmony into the physical body, and also reacts on your surroundings, your outer life.

If you concentrate on trouble, you will surely get it. If you persistently concentrate on the outworking of good, God's purpose will reveal itself to you as wise and loving. It is perfectly automatic; it is a law of life; as a person thinks, so he is, so she becomes. As you think in your meditation, as you create pictures through your imagination, you manipulate finer forces, finer ethers. You are creating your particular forms from the substance of the invisible worlds.

Whatever you think, you become. What you see in your surroundings, in your work, in your religion; whatever it is you create, you are in it. Then it either holds you prisoner and enslaves you, or if your thoughts are God-thoughts, you are released; you are free. You are your own jailer, your own liberator.

You will see why it is so important for you to

learn the lesson of self-control and self-discipline if you would enjoy perfect health, live an ordered life in beauty and harmony. Indeed, the very first step for any soul is to discipline itself. Discipline means strict obedience to the law of God. God is the law. God has given everyone understanding of this. Every living soul has access to this inner knowledge. God has implanted the still small voice within all; but at humanity's present stage of development, people prefer not to listen. If everyone obeyed the voice of God, then human kind would be saved. This sounds old-fashioned, but it is the truth and the key, for within that still small voice lies the creative power of love.

Healing with Thought

Spiritual healing is brought about through aspiration. When the thoughts are truly aspiring to the Christ, then the light of Christ shines into the heart. These rays of Christ Light, having great power, can reverse the order of things. Darkness and disease showing in the physical body can be changed; the light takes possession, dominating the body and controlling the physical atoms. Thus miracles are performed. When we say that thought has the power to do this, we of course mean the divine thought, the thought arising from a pure and aspiring heart. The power that comes when the heart is set on God can reverse negative to positive, darkness to light. This will come in the future; the inflowing of the light will produce perfect health.

There are still lessons to be learnt, however; there is so much to be learnt by the soul, so much work to be done in a physical body. Earth is like a school, but it is progressive, and as the soul returns in succeeding incarnations it passes all the classes and in due course graduates through the university and becomes a master.

We have spoken of the Christ Circle and the urgent necessity that groups of people should be active mentally, working for reconstruction in the new age. We pointed out the importance of positive, good thought: so many people are as careless in their thinking as in their speaking, not realizing the power behind thought as well as words. They think critically of others, not understanding that every soul needs the help of constructive, positive thought. When people hurl critical and destructive thoughts at each other, they are pulling their companions down and hurting them.

We have often spoken of the overcoming and abolition of cruelty in the new age, and when we do so you immediately think of cruelty to animals. But this is only one aspect of cruelty. The abolition of destructive and cruel thought is as important as the abolition of cruelty to animals and their slaughter. We are aware that constructive criticism has its place. To some degree it can stimulate and lead perhaps to the perfecting of a work. But there is a fine line of distinction between suggestions that are construc-tive and helpful, and critical, antagonistic thought. We want, however, to make the point that creative good thought is God thought.

Some of your leaders are great souls in a position of authority and bear a grave responsibility, but they are hindered in their work by the criticism of others. If people only understood this, they would surely help their leaders by projecting goodwill and kind-ness to them, and by surrounding them with the light of Christ. Good thought, God thought, is positive thought. All good leaders everywhere should con-tinually be supported and helped by good thought.

Think of the radiation of thought. Human kind

is overcoming space and time through the discovery of the secrets of nature. You regard the reception of sound and the light waves across the ether as an ordinary occurrence. In the comparatively near future, when men and women develop inner powers, they will regard the conscious reception of thought-waves in the same way. You could receive these thought-waves now if you were trained and practised for this purpose. Your soul, your psyche, is the sensitive instrument; it is continually receiving impressions of human thought-waves quite unconsciously. This is why so many people suffer through their nervous system, which interpenetrates the higher etheric and the soul body. People who are striving to unfold or develop their psychic powers, their means of spiritual perception, are advised to keep away from humanity *en masse* as far as possible. It is a great trial for a sensitive to have to enter, say, a crowded theatre, a cinema, or to mix with crowds. Those of you who live in the city know how weary you get, without understanding why you are so depleted or why you long to withdraw. When you reach the country, you begin to respond to the healing vibrations of nature.

Now when you begin to realize what you are contending with in daily life it will perhaps encourage you to train yourselves to project only kind and loving thought, for constructive thought, good thought, is your protection against the influence and penetration of negative or 'evil' thought. Moreover, every constructive, God-thought helps the whole of human kind to rise.

Together we work for the Future

A rapid development is taking place now, although humanity may be largely unconscious of it. In a little while the human race will be uplifted by its own effort and the effort of the hierarchies. There is also great spiritual activity in outer space, a penetration of the mists of earth by the angelic life. Human kind must learn to be receptive to these radiations from outer space. You must prepare yourselves by gentle, good thought, by abolishing all that is cruel, unseemly, ungodly, to receive visitors from other worlds, physical, etheric and spiritual. Moreover you have to become aware not only of the life in outer space and in other planets, but also of the conscious life in all nature, and your own relationship to it in every kingdom.

Think often of the Great Ones who in their

meditation and in their contemplation of humanity can help you and all souls. Of course they can come. That will depend on you. However simple you may be, however unworthy you may feel, if you sound your own keynote and it is harmonious, if your note is clear and true as a bell, it will echo in the Master's heart; you will call him and he will answer. *Ask, and it shall be given you; seek, and ye shall find*,* he told his disciples. There is nothing that you may not know if you seek in the right way. The truth about this universal spiritual life has been revealed to you. You have cried out to God. You have searched, you have longed for truth; and a little truth has been revealed in your own heart. You will meet other travellers on the path of life, many of whom will ask you for guidance. You can be a messenger to them. Do not hesitate to help them by word, deed and thought. Keep your vision on your goal, which is God, the eternal, everlasting Life.

A MOMENT OF REFLECTION

It is never easy to find words to convey our message, so we shall try to create a picture that will help you to receive ideas

*Matthew 7 : 7

we cannot adequately clothe in words.

We want to take you to a place in the world of light. Forget your body and your lower mind, and concentrate on the centre of light within your being; use your heavenly imagination to visualize a vast arena with seats or steps rising in tiers from the centre to an unimaginable height, even beyond your capacity to see. It is like an immense sun or circle of radiant light, most delicate, glowing with all the soft radiance of the spiritual heart of life....

You will see, as you gaze, that all those seats rising from the base and far beyond your vision are filled by a vast company of white-robed brethren; and among this great gathering there is a sense of expectancy. You will hear music . . . the harmony of the spheres.

Now, see coming down into your vision, the form of the simple, loving Master, the embodiment of the Cosmic Christ. Can you feel and respond to his blessing? Do you see the beauty of his face, the simplicity and nobility of his bearing, the wisdom and love that shines from him? Do you feel his love drawing you towards him, giving you peace, reassurance, strength? What matters the outer world where the children of life play, for here, in this amphitheatre, there is infinite power and love, the centre of divine will.

Oh, do you feel the enfoldment of this love? In this you can consciously live, and from this centre you go forth to

serve your brethren and all life. He, the gentle Master, knows.
He will give you the wisdom to act rightly.
Hold this vision quietly and steadily for thirty
seconds, if you can, and you will receive the blessing. . . .
O Great Spirit! Thy blessing upon Thy children is
great. Humbly we offer our hearts in Thy service. May the
peace and love of the eternal truth bless this earth and turn all
human thoughts away from destruction onto the true path of
helping others.

Amen.

THE WHITE EAGLE PUBLISHING TRUST, which publishes and distributes the White Eagle teaching, is part of the wider work of the White Eagle Lodge, a present-day mystery school in which people may find a place for growth and understanding, and a place in which the teachings of White Eagle find practical expression. Here men and women may come to learn the reason for their life on earth and how to serve and live in harmony with the whole brotherhood of life, visible and invisible, in health and happiness. The White Eagle Publishing Trust website is at www.whiteaglepublishing.org.

Readers wishing to know more of the work of the White Eagle Lodge may write to the General Secretary, The White Eagle Lodge, New Lands, Brewells Lane, Liss, Hampshire, England GU33 7HY (tel. 01730 893300) or can call at The White Eagle Lodge, 9 St Mary Abbots Place, Kensington, London W8 6LS (tel. 020-7603 7914). In the Americas please write to The Church of the White Eagle Lodge at P. O. Box 930, Montgomery, Texas 77356 (tel. 936-597 5757), and in Australasia to The White Eagle Lodge (Australasia), P. O. Box 225, Maleny, Queensland 4552, Australia (tel. 07-5494 4397).

Our websites and email addresses are as follows.
www.whiteagle.org; enquiries@whiteagle.org (worldwide);
www.whiteaglelodge.org; sjrc@whiteaglelodge.org (Americas);
www.whiteagle.ca (Canada); and www.whiteeaglelodge.org.au;
enquiries@whiteeaglelodge.org.au (Australasia)